Preparing
to
Preach

Barry Glendinning

NOVALIS

THE LITURGICAL PRESS

Design: Eye-to-Eye Design, Toronto

Layout: Suzanne Latourelle

Illustrations: Eugene Kral

Series Editor: Bernadette Gasslein

© 1997, Novalis, Saint Paul University, Ottawa, Ontario, Canada

Business Office: Novalis, 49 Front Street East, 2nd floor, Toronto, Ontario M5E 1B3

Published in the United States of America by The Liturgical Press, Box 7500, Collegeville, MN 56321-7500

Novalis: ISBN 2 89088 807 x

The Liturgical Press: ISBN 0-8146-2508-8
A Liturgical Press Book
Library of Congress data available on request.

Printed in Canada

Glendinning, Barry
Preparing to preach

(Preparing for liturgy)
Includes bibliographical references.

ISBN 2-89088-807-X

1. Catholic preaching. 2. Catholic Church–Liturgy. I. Title. II. Series.

BX1756.A1G54 1997   251   C97-900970-7

Contents

✓ p 29
✓ p. 30

Introduction

The liturgical renewal launched by the Second Vatican Council is the most ambitious and dramatic reform of the liturgy ever undertaken by the church. Already, within the first half-century after the council, its effects are being felt everywhere.

From the beginning, the goal of the liturgical renewal has been clear. The *Constitution on the Sacred Liturgy (CSL)* addressed the question as follows: "The Church earnestly desires that all the faithful be led to that full, conscious, and active participation in liturgical celebrations called for by the very nature of the liturgy ... In the reform and promotion of the liturgy, this full and active participation by all the people is the aim to be considered before all else" (14).

The church has been prepared to invest so much time and effort in liturgical renewal because it recognizes the supreme importance of the assembly's participation in the sacred mysteries. Genuine participation in the liturgy constantly renews the church and gives it the vitality it needs to evangelize the world. As the *CSL* puts it, "the liturgy is the summit toward which the activity of the church is directed; at the same time it is the fount from which all the church's power flows" (10).

To achieve its goal of full, conscious and active participation, the council reached back to the time when popular participation flourished, thus reclaiming the riches of the past. The language of the people, the general intercessions, the greeting of peace and communion from the cup are examples that readily spring to mind.

The homily is one of the principal liturgical actions restored by the council. Its importance within the broad picture of liturgical renewal is indicated by the language of the *Constitution:* "... as part of the liturgy itself therefore, the homily is strongly recommended; in fact, at Masses celebrated with the assistance of the people on Sundays and holy days of obligation, it is not to be omitted except for a serious reason" (52).

It may well be that the homily is the key element of the entire reform. Some observers have argued that twenty-five or thirty years of good homilies will do more to revitalize the church than anything else one can imagine. It is with this in mind that we offer this book as a service to homilists everywhere. Our hope is that, in its own small way, it will advance the renewal of the church and the evangelization of the world during this exciting age of the Second Vatican Council.

CHAPTER 1

What Is Liturgical Preaching?

The documents of the Second Vatican Council do not give us a detailed picture of the homily, so we have to go searching for an answer to the question: What is liturgical preaching?

From the time of the homily's reappearance in the liturgy, at least one thing has been clear: the homily is not a sermon.

The sermon was understood to be a break or interruption in the celebration of mass. It was basically an instruction on some aspect of the church's faith. Some dioceses had an organized preaching agenda—one year on the creed, another on the ten commandments.

The homily is the original form of preaching from which the sermon eventually emerged during a period of liturgical decline. Unlike the sermon, the homily is an integral part of the liturgy and is rooted in the scriptural readings of the day.

Keeping this distinction in mind, we can turn our attention to the homily itself and to its place within the church's witness to the word of God.

Since the homily is a very specific item on the church's preaching agenda, we'll approach it by way of a series of snapshots, beginning with a wide-angle picture and then gradually narrowing the field to the homily itself:

- snapshot 1: the preached word
- snapshot 2: the liturgical setting
- snapshot 3: the dynamics of encounter
- snapshot 4: the homily

Snapshot 1: The Preached Word

Our wide-angle snapshot focuses our attention on the word "preach." Its Latin root is *praedicare*, which means "to proclaim." Thus, whoever preaches proclaims a word or a message; the message that the church's herald proclaims can be nothing other than the gospel of Jesus Christ, the good news of the kingdom of God.

The paschal mystery

This gospel is the good news of Jesus' rising from the dead and his ascension into Spirit-filled glory. It is the good news of his sending of the Holy Spirit, who draws the world into the Lord's own kingdom life.

In brief, the gospel is the good news of Jesus' passage to the life of the kingdom and of the world's passage in him. It is the good news of the world's salvation. This paschal mystery lies at the heart of the church's proclamation. The church proclaims a paschal faith, celebrates a paschal liturgy, and lives a paschal life. The passover, or the passage into the life of the kingdom of God, is the centre of it all.

The prophetic church

Looking more closely at our snapshot, we see that all of us are responsible for this preaching. The church is a prophetic community; it speaks on behalf of the Lord. All members of the people of God bear witness to the good news and reveal the paschal mystery to the world. The bishop is the first carrier of this word, mobilizes its proclamation, and ensures its authenticity, but the whole church is the herald.

Variations on a theme

Finally, we notice that the church's preaching takes various forms depending on the circumstances of those who hear it.

When the church proclaims the good news to those who have not yet heard it, we call this preaching *evangelization*. Its purpose is to dispose the hearers to initial faith.

The church then turns to *catechesis*. Catechesis re-echoes the good news, fills out its setting within the great story of God, and supports its proper understanding with doctrinal teachings.

The third form of preaching the good news is called *paraclesis*. This is the ongoing proclamation of the good news within the community that believes, cherishes, and lives the paschal mystery. It is here that liturgical preaching finds its place.

Whether it is evangelization, catechesis or paraclesis, the preached word is always the good news of salvation. The contexts are different, but the basic content is invariably the same: the good news of the passover of the Lord and the passage of the world—through, with and in him—into the kingdom of God.

Snapshot 2: The Liturgical Setting

We have seen that liturgical preaching falls within the broad category we call *paraclesis*: the ongoing proclamation of the good news within the community that already lives the mystery of Christ. But liturgical preaching is more specific than that. Liturgical preaching takes place within the church's sacramental events. Above all, it takes place within the church's fundamental act of self-realization, the celebration of the eucharist. We need, then, to examine the homily's eucharistic setting.

Fulfilled in your hearing

The eucharist is celebrated within new time—the time of the recreation of the world in Christ, the time of the coming of the kingdom of God. The eucharist is that crucial event that draws the world here and now into the passage of Jesus Christ to the kingdom of the Father. It is the Passover meal of the New Testament times.

Within this setting, the homily stands out as the church's most astonishing proclamation of the gospel of Jesus Christ. It proclaims the paschal mystery as filled out and accomplished in the lives of those who take part in this very celebration: "Today this scripture has been fulfilled in your hearing" (Lk 4:21).

Snapshot 3: The Dynamics of Encounter

Our third snapshot takes us into the inner workings of the church's eucharist. Three aspects of the celebration draw our particular attention: the assembly, the liturgy of the word and the liturgy of the eucharist.

The assembly

The Sunday assembly has always been the fundamental and most dramatic feature of the church's life. This is because the assembly is the Lord's own undertaking for the reconstruction of the world: "And I, when I am lifted up from the earth, will draw all people to myself" (Jn 12:32); "And the one who was seated on the throne said, 'See, I am making all things new'" (Rv 21:5).

Thus it is the exalted Lord of glory who even now, in the age of fulfillment, gathers the world together in the power of the Holy Spirit. The Sunday assembly is an event of God in the life of the world.

The liturgy of the word

Set within the dynamics of the Lord's assembly, the liturgy of the word is charged with special power. The word of God comes alive in our midst as an invitation to share in the blessing of kingdom life today. For the Christian community, the people assembled in the Lord, this gracious call of God makes the liturgy of the word a grand celebration of the message of salvation.

The liturgy of the word opens up a dialogue of love between God and the world; God's invitation, given by the risen and exalted Lord, is intended to evoke a heartfelt "Yes," within this very event, to the gracious gift of new life in Christ.

The liturgy of the eucharist

God's invitation to share new life in Christ is fulfilled even now within the eucharistic celebration. The Lord has set a festive table in our midst, the table of the feast of the kingdom of God; he provides us with the food and drink of everlasting life; he draws us into his own communion of life in the triune God.

In the eucharistic prayer, the assembly joins the exalted Lord in praying the table blessing of the kingdom feast. Here, in this prayer, the world responds to the wondrous divine initiative: a grand hymn of thanksgiving, a joyful song in which it offers the whole of its life to the glory of God.

Then, in the church's consummate act, the assembly shares the food and drink of the festive table, participating in the body and blood of Christ and rejoicing in communion of life in the triune God.

Snapshot 4: The Homily

In our first snapshot, we saw that the homily is part of a wide range of preaching that is invariably centred on the paschal mystery of Jesus Christ. It belongs to that kind of preaching called *paraclesis*: the ongoing proclamation of the good news within the community that believes, cherishes and lives the mystery that is proclaimed.

Our second snapshot focused on the special setting of the homily. The homily takes place within the eucharist, the grand event that draws the world into the paschal mystery itself. Hence, liturgical preaching proclaims the good news as accomplished in our midst.

In our third snapshot, we saw that the homily stands within a living dialogue between God and the world. In the liturgy, the word is alive and active, inviting the assembly to share the mystery of Christ's passage to glorious and lordly life by participating in the banquet feast of the kingdom.

Our final snapshot focuses on the homily itself. It lets us see the function of the homily within the liturgy of the word and within the living dialogue of the eucharistic celebration.

The bishop or presbyter speaks on behalf of Christ

The bishop or presbyter proclaims the good news as a living message given to the world today. He does this as the sacramental icon of Christ, for the Lord himself presides and is present in the word proclaimed.

The same message echoes throughout the ages

The bishop speaks as one who stands in the long line of apostolic succession. It is his responsibility to hand on faithfully what he himself has received as coming from the apostles. Thus, in the homily, the bishop continues throughout succeeding generations the church's oral transmission of the gospel and its call to kingdom life.

At its heart and centre, the apostolic witness is invariably the same. The homily builds upon the scriptural proclamations of the day and unfolds the perennial good news of Jesus Christ, who even now calls the world to communion of life in God.

In Summary

1. The homily is the highest form of the church's witness to the gospel of Jesus Christ. Set within the church's officially constituted assembly, it announces the good news of the kingdom of God as fulfilled in our midst even as we listen.

2. Its goal is to build up the community once again as an assembly of living faith—an assembly whose eyes are open to the wonder of the moment, an assembly that stands in awe before the mighty works of God, that savours the presence of the Lord of glory, that cherishes the living call to kingdom life, that is eager to respond to God's gracious invitation and to gather at the table of the feast, that drinks deeply of the mystery that is celebrated, and that enters more fully than ever into the joy of the Lord.

3. The homily is the church's faithful witness. It is the Lord's amazing revelation that today is the day of salvation, that even now, in this age of fulfillment, the reign of God is established in the world. Seized anew by this revelation, the assembly is led to proclaim with open heart, "This day was made by the Lord; we rejoice and are glad" (responsorial psalm, Easter Sunday).

Discussion Questions

1. How would you describe the difference between a sermon and a homily?

2. Unlike the sermon, the homily is an integral part of the celebration. The homily and its counterpart, the eucharistic prayer, are liturgical acts that are the responsibility of the one who presides. What are your thoughts on the practice, common in the age of the sermon, of a presbyter (priest) other than the presider giving the homily?

CHAPTER 2

From Principles to Texts

The Bible is the book of the church, and it is within the great assembly that it finds its vital place. In the midst of the community of believers, the word is proclaimed as a living reality in the world today. Here, the word is explained in terms of its deepest meaning for the life of the gathered church. Here, the homilist unfolds the gospel as fulfilled even as we listen.

In this chapter, we examine some examples of how the homilist can reach into the scriptural proclamations and extract their life-giving meaning for the liturgical assembly today.

Matthew 20:1-16

On the twenty-fifth Sunday in ordinary time, year A, the gospel is about the landowner who invites workers into his vineyard. At the end of the day, he pays each of them a day's wage, beginning with the last to come.

This gospel is at first perplexing. If we view it from the perspective of social justice, it seems to be all wrong. All the workers get the same wage regardless of the number of hours they have worked; the last to come are paid first!

But Jesus tells us that this is a parable about the kingdom. In the parable, then, God is the "landowner" and the vineyard is an image of the kingdom. The parable presents a warm picture of the gracious God who again and again goes in search of the people of the world, urging them to share the new life which Christ has won for them.

The "pay" is the same for all of them regardless of when they respond, even if it is at the eleventh hour of their lives. What is offered to one and all is communion of life in God forever. The first reading (Is 55:6-9) is, as always, a related text: "Seek the Lord while he may be found ..."

But when the gospel is proclaimed in the liturgical assembly there is always much more: there is an immediacy, a "nowness" to the sacred texts, for they are announced as fulfilled in us even as we listen.

Today God's call touches this assembly. Today God invites this assembly to share the life of the kingdom, to live the life of Jesus, the risen Lord of glory. Today God invites this assembly to the table of the paschal feast. Today this assembly shares communion of life in the triune God.

Reading the scriptures in this way, the homilist becomes a living witness to the church's paschal faith, a revealer of the sacred mysteries, a herald of the kingdom unfolding in the world today, a celebrant of the mighty acts of God accomplished even as we listen.

Matthew 11:2-11

On the third Sunday in Advent, year A, the gospel records an event involving John the Baptist and Jesus. From prison, John sends his disciples to ask Jesus a question: "Are you the one who is to come, or are we to wait for another?"

John's question was asked long ago, but it echoes throughout the whole of human history. It is, in fact, the quintessential question that challenges the world in every generation. Even today it has to be answered; on the answer hangs the destiny of the nations.

For the liturgical assembly, the answer is clear. Our gathering on the day of the resurrection vibrantly witnesses to the truth that Jesus is the long-awaited One, the Messiah, the Saviour, the Lord of glory. With Paul we "confess that Jesus Christ is Lord to the glory of God the Father" (Ph 2:11).

This public witness on the Lord's Day "spills out" into the whole of our lives and colours everything we say and do. In all of our relationships, whether at home or at work or at school, and above all in our life together as the church of God, we stand under the lordship of Jesus Christ. Our abiding hope is that this living witness will lead the nations into the fullness of the truth.

The closing sentence of today's gospel helps us see the marvels of the eucharistic celebration: "Truly I tell you, among those born of women, no one has arisen greater than John the Baptist; yet the least in the kingdom of heaven is greater than he."

Is this saying not fulfilled in the assembly today? Today the Lord himself has gathered us together. The Lord presides, and is present in our midst. And the Lord is more than present; he shares his very life with us in holy communion. The Lord lives in us and we in him. At the table of the feast we are fashioned into his very body and become the living temple of the Holy Spirit. Let us cherish the moment and rejoice in the Lord.

Mark 7:31-37

On the twenty-third Sunday in ordinary time, year B, the gospel records Jesus' healing of a "deaf man who had an impediment in his speech." What Jesus did was truly extraordinary: "He took him aside in private, away from the crowd, and put his fingers into his ears, and he spat and touched his tongue. Then looking up to heaven, he sighed and said to him, 'Ephphatha,' that is, 'Be opened.' And immediately his ears were opened, his tongue was released, and he spoke plainly."

Does this event not remind us of our Christian initiation? Did the Lord not take us aside, into the precincts of his body, the church? There, in the power of his own Holy Spirit, did he not heal our deafness so that we now hear with faith the living word of salvation? Did he not loosen our tongues so that we now find a voice for praise and thanksgiving to the glory of God? Surely this is what those events we call baptism and confirmation really mean.

Because the Lord's healing power has touched not only the man in the gospel text but our lives as well, we can stand in the church's assembly today, celebrating God's mighty acts and offering our heartfelt praise and thanksgiving for the wonderful gift of new and everlasting life.

Luke 12:13-21

On the eighteenth Sunday in ordinary time, year C, Jesus tells the parable of the rich farmer who had an exceptional harvest. The man said to himself: "I will pull down my barns and build larger ones, and there I will store all my grain and my goods. And I will say to my soul, 'Soul, you have ample goods laid up for many years; relax, eat, drink, be merry.'"

God's answer is abrupt: "You fool! This very night your life is being demanded of you. And the things you have prepared, whose will they be?" Jesus' conclusion is equally straightforward: "So it is with those who store up treasures for themselves but are not rich toward God."

At first sight, this gospel seems to provide an opportunity for the homilist to urge the assembly to take the Lord's warning to heart and to set its sights on the kingdom of heaven. Moralizing admonitions of this kind, however, do not fit the context of the liturgical celebration. Let's look at that context once again.

The homily takes place within the assembled church. Now, the church is by definition the community that has already embraced the kingdom of heaven. It lives this mystery, and it has come together precisely to celebrate it anew. It has already heeded the Lord's injunction to be rich toward God. This is why it can recognize his message as good news for the world today.

The role of the homilist, then, is to voice the assembled church's living faith: What Jesus says is indeed true. What counts is to be "rich toward God." Our constant assembling on the day of the resurrection publicly testifies to this truth. In the Sunday eucharist, we proclaim again and again that our life is in God. From Sunday to Sunday we profess that to God belongs the glory and the honour for ever and ever. Our true and only riches lie in communion of life in the triune God. That is why we are always eager to celebrate the feast.

Thus the homily supports and strengthens the life of the church, not by its moral admonitions, but by its faithful witness to the truth that the community already professes and holds close to its heart.

And there is more. The eucharist is the fundamental covenant-making event of the church. In the liturgy of the word, God issues anew the invitation to share the glorious life of the Lord. In the liturgy of the eucharist, the assembly responds to this divine call, offering, in the eucharistic prayer, the gift of its own life in thanksgiving to God. This covenantal exchange is then sealed and ratified in holy communion. Hence, in the eucharist our covenant with God is made and constantly renewed; in the eucharist, we become the people of the covenant, the New Testament church.

We can see from this that the church's moral life is rooted in the eucharistic celebration. This event binds God and the world together in a covenant of shared life and love, and informs the whole of our Christian lives.

The homilist will take this extraordinary setting into account, encouraging the assembly to pray the eucharistic prayer with ever greater fervour, to seal the covenant in holy communion with ever greater openness of heart, to enter ever more deeply into covenant life, to make itself ever richer in the sight of God.

In Summary

1. The homily is the highest form of the church's preaching. Its context is the officially constituted assembly of the church. Its methodology is to explain, interpret, unfold the scriptural readings as fulfilled even as we listen.

2. Its character is witness, revelation, proclamation, celebration.

3. Its goal is to build and rebuild the assembly as the covenanted people of God, the community of glorious kingdom life. It will give way, in the fulfillment of the age, to the unbounded and everlasting praise of God.

Discussion Questions

1. The liturgical method of interpreting the scriptural proclamations is rooted in the extraordinary setting of the church's celebrations. Are the paschal or kingdom dimensions of the liturgy generally taken into account in our preaching today?

2. What are your thoughts on the practice of setting the homily aside from time to time in favour of a report, an appeal for funds, or some other kind of presentation?

CHAPTER 3

Getting Ready to Preach

Every homilist develops a particular way of getting ready to preach. This chapter makes some basic suggestions that can help refine the process.

Settling into the Project

Presiders are usually very busy people; all kinds of demands are made upon their time. It's important, then, to block out sufficient time to prepare the homily well.

Begin your preparation early in the week, on Monday if possible, and spend some time each day with the Lectionary texts. Don't rush the process, and give plenty of room for the Holy Spirit to guide your reflection.

Working with the Lectionary

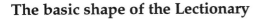

The Lectionary that was produced after the Second Vatican Council is a rich resource for liturgical preaching. Homilists should study the introductory material to gain a clear understanding of the way that the Lectionary is arranged. (For more on this topic, see *Preparing the Table of the Word* in this series.)

The basic shape of the Lectionary

The *Constitution on the Sacred Liturgy* called for the fuller use of scripture in the church's liturgy: "The treasures of the Bible are to be opened up more lavishly, so that a richer share in God's word may be provided for the faithful. In this way a more representative portion of holy Scripture will be read to the people in the course of a prescribed number of years" (51).

With the publication of the Lectionary, the church returned to its venerable tradition of proclaiming three readings at the Sunday eucharist and gave fresh attention to the sung psalm. At the same time, it introduced a three-year cycle of Sunday readings based on the gospels according to Matthew, Mark and Luke. These gospels are read in a semi-continuous way in the course of their respective years.

The Hebrew scriptures, which comprise the first reading except during the Easter Season, are far too extensive to be presented in a semi-continuous manner, even within a three-year cycle. Because of this, the texts for the first reading were selected with a view to their correspondence with the gospel proclamation. This arrangement highlights the unity of the Old and New Testaments in the history of salvation.

The second reading (from the apostles) records the continued proclamation and living out of the good news in the early church. During ordinary time, the second reading follows its own semi-continuous pattern and is not directly related to the gospel text. During the seasons, however, it has been chosen to complement the gospel.

Reflecting on the readings

With the overall arrangement of the Lectionary in mind, we can suggest some practical applications:

1. Before each new liturgical year begins, spend some time reflecting on the particular synoptic gospel that will be proclaimed. Matthew, Mark and Luke present the good news in their own particular ways, giving a unique flavour to each cycle of celebrations. You will need to take this into account when you are preparing to preach.

2. Because the gospel text is presented in a semi-continuous way, you will need to situate the gospel text of any given Sunday within the wider sequence of lectionary readings.

3. When you turn your attention to a particular Sunday, it is a good idea to begin with a reflection on all the texts of the day (the opening prayer, and so on); together they provide a kind of panoramic view of the celebration.

4. When you begin to study the readings themselves, keep in mind that the gospel is the foundational text. Since the first reading (and sometimes the second) has been chosen because of its correspondence with the gospel, it will provide some insight into the particular aspect of the gospel text that is being highlighted today. Study it with this in mind. The Lectionary's brief comments at the head of each text will help as well.

Developing Your Homily

Here are some steps that you can take when you begin to prepare the homily itself. Since examples are often helpful, we shall use the readings from year C for the sixteenth Sunday in ordinary time. A resource that uses a similar approach in its commentaries on the scriptures is the periodical, *Celebrate!*, published by Novalis.

The gospel text (Lk 10:38-42) deals with Jesus' visit with Martha and Mary. Martha was "distracted by her many tasks," while Mary "sat at the Lord's feet." The first reading (Gn 18:1-10a) records Abraham's hospitality to the three men who visited him by the oaks of Mamre. The second reading (Col 1:24-28) reminds the Colossians that Paul became a servant of the church "to make the word of God fully known, the mystery that has been hidden throughout the ages and generations but has now been revealed to his saints."

Step 1: Examine the text at a basic level.

The setting of today's gospel is clear enough. Jesus is visiting at

Martha's house in Bethany, where he usually stays when he is in the vicinity of Jerusalem.

At first reading, the story seems to focus on a question of ordinary hospitality. Hospitality requires two things: the hosts have to prepare the food and set the table, and they have to enter into conversation with the guest. Both are equally important. Martha seems to be doing the one, and Mary the other.

But as usual, Luke throws a twist into the story, and we can be sure that it is deliberate. When Martha complains about having to do everything herself, Jesus replies, "Mary has chosen the better part ..."

Step 2: Draw the text into the paschal mystery.

What does Jesus mean when he says that Mary has chosen the better part? The question takes us to the heart of the matter. Jesus is no ordinary guest. He is the very Word become flesh. He brings the one message that the whole of the world must hear—the message of salvation.

When Jesus arrives, the usual rules of hospitality no longer apply. Only one thing counts, and that is to hear what Jesus has to say. When Jesus arrives, everything else is an unnecessary worry and a distraction.

Thus, Mary has chosen the better part. In fact, when Luke records that Mary "sat at the Lord's feet and listened to what he was saying," he is telling us that Mary has become the Lord's disciple.

Step 3: Move forward to today's celebration.

When the gospel is proclaimed in the eucharistic assembly, it is a living word given to us today. In a very real way, then, we are the Marthas and the Marys of the text.

Today we are the people who gather in the presence of the Lord. For us, as for Martha and Mary, there is only one thing that counts: to hear what the Lord has to say. Is the singing too slow or too fast? Is the building too cold or too hot? Do the servers seem to know what they are doing? All these questions (at this point, at least) are nothing more than needless worries and idle distractions.

In the first reading, Abraham recognized the appearance of the Lord in the three men who visited him as he sat at the entrance of his tent. He welcomes them with traditional and generous hospitality. When the Lord visits us, today's disciples of the Lord, we show our hospitality by sitting at the feet of the Word made flesh.

The remarkable message that Jesus brings to us today is the Father's invitation to share Jesus' risen and glorious life forever. In fact, the Lord has set the festive table of the kingdom in our very midst and invites us to eat and drink the bread and cup of everlasting life.

Only one thing counts for us who are disciples of the Lord: to hear what he has to say and to rejoice in the gift of God.

St. Paul, in his letter to the Colossians, says: "God chose to make known how great among the Gentiles are the riches of the glory of this mystery, which is Christ in you, the hope of glory." This mystery made known to us today is this mystery in which we share.

Reflections on the Process

The critical feature of the process is the movement, step by step, from the basic event described in the text to its meaning within the paschal mystery and then on to its significance within the eucharistic assembly today.

When the homily reveals the liturgical meaning of the sacred texts, it becomes the turning point of the liturgy of the word. The assembly, recognizing the scriptural proclamations as fulfilled in its hearing, marvels anew at God's mighty works, recognizes the mystery of salvation celebrated in its midst, and moves forward with conviction and joy to the table blessing of the paschal feast and communion of life in the triune God.

Proclaimed in this way from Sunday to Sunday, the homily

secures the great story of salvation as the foundation of the assembly's life. It is thus a key element in the ongoing renewal of the people of God as they journey toward the everlasting Day of the Lord.

In Summary

1. Presiders need free time to prepare their homilies. Block off some hours in your appointment book, beginning with Monday, and ease your way into the texts. Include time for reflection and prayer.

2. The Lectionary is the richest resource we have ever had for liturgical preaching. Presiders are encouraged to befriend it and give it a welcome home.

3. The Lectionary presents a highly organized sequence of readings. Here are some suggestions for presiders: Remember the particular characteristics of this year's gospel series (Matthew, Mark or Luke); examine the progress of the readings from last Sunday to this Sunday and the next; and then study the ways in which the first and second readings may be connected with the gospel.

4. Every eucharist is the celebration of the paschal mystery. Presiders should reflect on how Sunday's gospel is related to this mystery and how it applies to the celebrating church today.

Discussion Questions

1. As an integral part of the liturgy, the homily a) builds upon the scriptural proclamations of the day and b) leads forward to the eucharistic prayer and holy communion. Which of these two links do you think is more in need of development in our celebrations today?

2. Given the prophetic nature of the homily, what would you consider to be the appropriate use of homiletic aids? Would you use a "packaged" homily?

CHAPTER 4

The Art of Preaching

Every homilist needs particular skills in conversation and communication. All of these skills can be applied to liturgical preaching: the church's great venture of telling the story of salvation.

From Sunday to Sunday, homilists relate this story that lies at the heart of the church's life. Homilists, then, are the great story tellers of the community. It is always the same story that they tell, for only the story of Jesus' passage to glorious kingdom life and of the world's passage in him is valid for all peoples in all times; but it is always told from a 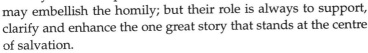 different starting point and in a slightly different way. Various experiences and other stories may embellish the homily; but their role is always to support, clarify and enhance the one great story that stands at the centre of salvation.

Good storytellers hold the attention of their listeners. When the great story is told well, it captures the imagination, fascinates the mind, delights the heart, and draws listeners in. This is what liturgical preaching should do.

The Sunday assembly is a wild and woolly mix of people: the young and the old, the educated and the uneducated are all there. But everybody loves a story; the story you tell is as simple as it is profound. Your story has the power to charm the whole world.

In this chapter, we'll make some basic suggestions that you may wish to keep in mind as you apply your skills to telling the story:

- Listen to the word;
- Try preaching from the chair;
- Speak from the heart;
- Respect the assembly;
- Always bring good news.

Listen to the Word

Let's presume that the Sunday eucharist is already underway and that the readings are being proclaimed. At this point you might run into a bit of a problem: you find yourself concentrating so much on what you are going to say that you're not really paying attention to what is going on in the celebration now.

On the surface it might seem that this little distraction doesn't really matter. After all, you've been mulling over the readings all week long. You know them like the back of your hand! But that would be a mistake.

When you settle into the liturgy of the word, it's a good idea to keep the special dynamics of the celebration in mind. You are sitting in the midst of the Sunday assembly, where the Spirit breathes with recreative energy and power; Christ himself is present in the word proclaimed. What is going on is nothing less than a living encounter with the God of salvation. All of this means that the proclamations claim our special attention; it means that the homilist, like everyone else in the assembly, needs to drink deeply of the word that is being announced here and now.

This reflection raises an interesting point: you should not have your homily so cast in stone that the Spirit, hovering over the assembly, cannot touch your proclamation today. It may be a bit scary to think about it, but the Spirit may lead you in a direction you did not expect!

Try Preaching from the Chair

You may preach from the chair or from the lectern. Allow us to suggest the chair. What is more, try preaching seated in the chair!

But why the chair? Because the chair is the teaching chair of Jesus Christ; when you preach, you preach in the name of the Lord. That's what it means to preside. To preside (from the Latin *praesedere*) means to assume the chair—to sit in front of the assembly.

There are two major advantages to preaching from the chair. The first has to do with being in the right place at the right time. If the chair is the teaching chair of Jesus Christ, and if you're speaking officially in his name, then the chair is where you belong.

The second advantage has to do with your rapport with the assembly. Sitting is the right posture for giving a household talk. It's a non-aggressive posture: you're sitting like everyone else. There is no suggestion that you are trying to dominate the assembly. It's the proper posture of conversation and sharing. Experience has shown that the seated posture has a dramatic effect on a person's style of preaching.

Naturally, all of this depends on the location of the chair. It ought to be located in the optimum place for you to preside. It's always unfortunate when the presider has to leave the chair to preside well.

One final suggestion about the chair: if you are going to use it for preaching, don't put a lectern in front of it; you will want an open and unencumbered space from which to speak to the assembly.

Speak from the Heart

What you bring is a witness—a living, apostolic witness to the good news of Jesus Christ. It's about an event that you yourself hold dearly, an event that is the substance of your life. Your witness is intended to inspire the assembly in the power of the Holy Spirit. What you say has to come from the depths of your whole being; it has to come from the heart.

Since the homily is a witness, you need to speak directly to the assembly. It's better, then, to set aside your written text, if you have one; and it's better to set aside your notes as well! After all, you don't have to entertain a crowd; you just have to tell the story from your heart.

It may seem to be a rather bold move to speak without a text. Perhaps the word "homily" can help us here. The word "homily" refers to a familiar conversation given in a gathering or an assembly. It brings us back to an understanding of the church as the household or family of God. It reminds us that the Sunday eucharist is a family event and that everybody in the assembly is our brother and our sister in Christ. Thinking "family" will help every homilist feel much more at ease in the celebration.

One final consideration deserves our attention. We have seen that liturgical preaching is a living, apostolic witness to the good news of Jesus Christ and that it engages the homilist's whole being. But here we have to make an important, if subtle, distinction: homilists do not draw attention to themselves.

Homilists speak in the name of Jesus Christ; their only concern is to be faithful witnesses to the good news of salvation. This means that, while homilists invest their whole person in the homily, they focus the assembly's attention on the message, not on themselves.

Respect the Assembly

A unique feature of liturgical preaching is that it takes place in the community that already believes, cherishes and lives the good news of Jesus Christ. You give your homily in the midst of the holy people of God, the sacramental body of Christ, the living temple of the Holy Spirit. All of this suggests preaching that shows the deepest respect for the Lord's brothers and sisters.

For example, when you preach in the liturgical assembly, it's good to remember that you're not telling the people of God something that they don't already know. Rather, you're giving them a fresh and vibrant witness to the mystery that is even now the foundation and joy of their lives.

Here is another example. It's certainly true that the message you bring is given in the name of Jesus Christ, the Prophet, and that you speak in fulfillment of your prophetic office in the church. But at the same time it is equally true that you are preaching within an assembly that is itself a community of prophets, a people living in the grace and power of Holy Spirit.

A simple suggestion comes to mind. Sitting in the midst of the household, it seems to be a good idea to make ample use of the pronoun "we." For example: "Today we are gathered in the presence of the Lord ... Today God invites us to share in the mystery of salvation ... We are the people who are blessed by the Lord today."

This kind of language keeps you anchored within the assembly, where the homilist always belongs. It has the added advantage of drawing all the people into the story, which, after all, is their own. It is true that the homilist speaks as the sacramental icon of Christ, the head of his body, the church; but the head is never separated from the body!

Always Bring Good News

The church is a gospel community; its entire life is centred on the good news of salvation. Quite naturally, the homily echoes that good news in the Sunday eucharist. Moreover, good news begets joy; and this joy is perhaps the most precious and compelling feature of the church's new life. This joy likewise needs to find a home in liturgical preaching.

This is not to say that all our problems have suddenly gone away. To be sure, the struggle between light and darkness goes on in the world, in the Christian community, and in our own lives. But we know that Jesus Christ has already won the definitive struggle against the darkness. Even now, Jesus is Lord; in the end, his victory and triumph will be filled out in the whole world.

Perhaps even more to the point, the joy that comes from the good news of salvation has a special place in the celebration of the eucharist, where the assembly consorts with the risen Lord and revels in the experience of kingdom life. Here, in the eucharistic celebration, the assembly is at home with its God.

When you preach the homily, then, remember that you always bring good news and you bring it with particular joy. The conviction of your voice, the confidence of your words, and the joy of your expression should say it all.

In Summary

1. When you preside at the liturgy of the word, always give the scripture proclamations your full attention. The Spirit breathes within the assembly and draws us deeply into the wisdom of God.

2. Try preaching from the chair and without notes. If you feel some discomfort with the project, you may find it useful to begin with some weekday celebrations.

3. It is easier to give an instruction than to speak from the heart. But prayer and reflection during your homily preparation open the way to a living, embodied witness to the good news of salvation.

4. Remember that you are bearing witness to the church's faith in the midst of your brothers and sisters, the body of Christ. Always treat the assembly with the utmost respect.

5. In every age, the church brings good news, glad tidings, gospel. Always build up the community. Always bring joy.

Discussion Questions

1. Homilists should put their whole being into the homily without pointing to themselves. How do you see this principle working itself out in the homily?

2. The homily is addressed to the entire assembly, young and old alike. How would you tell the story of salvation in a way that would capture everyone's imagination? Do we really need a children's liturgy of the word on Sunday?

CHAPTER 5

Preaching throughout the Year

The liturgical year unfolds the paschal mystery one step at a time. The year begins with the celebration of Jesus' arrival and moves forward steadily to his passage to the Father. It concludes with the feast of Christ the King and the church's expectation of his final coming in glory.

Thus, as you preach throughout the liturgical year, you have an outstanding opportunity to highlight every aspect of the paschal mystery of Jesus Christ.

The Liturgical Year

Perhaps the best way to understand the liturgical year is to see it in terms of the church's journey to the Father.

The journey motif runs strong and deep through the paschal mystery. Jesus came to undertake on behalf of the whole world a journey that would take him through death and resurrection to the right hand of the Father. And Jesus said to his disciples, "Follow me" (Jn 21:19).

Each year, responding to this call, we travel with the Lord. In every age and until the end of time, we are the people of the journey. The liturgical year, which embodies that journey, is the framework of our spiritual lives.

Suggestions

- As you preach throughout the liturgical year, and as you highlight the various steps along the way, always keep the total journey in mind. Let's take, for example, the season of Advent. During Advent, you will be emphasizing the return and arrival of the Lord. At the same time, always remind the assembly that Jesus came to us to lead us back to the Father. Advent is part of the paschal mystery, and it points us forward to the Easter Triduum, the annual celebration of the passover of the Lord.
- Remember also that the homily leads the assembly forward to the liturgy of the eucharist, which is the paschal meal itself. Thus, to use Advent as an example once again, you should point the assembly forward to its actual participation in the passage to the Father as they celebrate the church's feast.

The liturgical year is "for real"

Our description of the liturgical year as the church's journey with Jesus to the Father raises an important question: Is the liturgical year "for real"? Is there really an arrival of the Lord, an epiphany of the Lord, and so on? The answer to this question will definitely affect your preaching.

The liturgical year is "for real" because the eucharist is "for real." For example, Advent is always a reality for the liturgical assembly, since, again and again, the Lord comes into its midst. The Lord gathers us together. The Lord speaks to us and leads us to the table of the feast. The Lord shares his life with us in holy communion. In truth, the Lord comes among us. In truth, we travel with the Lord.

Epiphany provides us with another example. At one level, it celebrates the showing forth of Jesus as Lord by the wise men and their gifts. At another level, it celebrates the showing forth of Jesus as Lord by this assembly and its gift of praise and thanksgiving. The epiphany of old, grand though it was, involved a few visitors from the East and their gifts of gold, frankincense and myrrh. Every Sunday eucharist is a far greater epiphany of the Lord, for it brings the public witness of assemblies throughout the world and the gift of their lives for the glory of God.

Advent

Advent is the beginning of the church's year of grace. Like any beginning, it should be marked by fresh excitement, energy, expectation and joy. Since the community is starting off on another leg of its journey with the Lord, it needs to pull itself together, shake off all its distractions, set its sights on its destination, and start out afresh, briskly and eagerly.

Suggestions

- Pick up on the excitement of a new beginning and draw the community together for a common undertaking: the journey to the kingdom of the Father.
- Celebrate Advent as a sacramental reality: every eucharist is the arrival of the Lord in our midst; he journeys with us and we journey in him.

Christmas

The entire Christmas season celebrates the incarnation of the Son of God and his manifestation to the world; it celebrates that grand exchange in which God becomes one with us that we may become one with God.

Christmas signals a new and glorious dignity for humankind: a dignity that is fulfilled in each one of us through our participation in the sacraments of Christian initiation, including, above all, the feast of passage into the life of the triune God. Christmas is a festival of the transformation of the world in Christ.

Suggestion

- At Christmas, remember that the church does not linger on the infant Jesus. After all, Jesus is now the risen and glorious Lord. The church's focus is the incarnation; here, in the incarnation, we recognize the connection between Christmas and the paschal mystery of Jesus Christ. The Word becomes flesh to lead us through death and resurrection to the life of glory, where we share in his divinity forever. This is what happens in the eucharist: God shares with us the life of Jesus, the Lord of glory.

Ordinary Time

The liturgical year originally consisted of a series of Sunday eucharists, each of them (as today) celebrating the total mystery of Christ. At a very early date, the Easter Triduum developed and became the focal point of the entire year. Then, gradually, various seasons, all of them related to the Triduum, were superimposed on the sequence of Sunday celebrations.

The seasons, however, do not cover the entire liturgical year, with the result that we still have thirty-three or thirty-four weeks that belong to the original series of Sunday celebrations. These weeks comprise Ordinary Time or the original, ordered (numbered) time of the church.

Thus, Ordinary Time is in no way "low" time that simply fills in the year between the seasons. In fact, the church's time is always extraordinary time: the new time of the coming of the kingdom of God.

Suggestions

- Ordinary Time is the time when the Lectionary sketches Jesus' public ministry and his journey to death and resurrection. As Jesus journeys, he proclaims the good news of the kingdom of God and gathers followers to himself. It's a good idea to keep the assembly in touch with its own journey in Jesus. It travels with him to the three-day feast of Christian passover and makes passage with him through death and resurrection to the life of the heavenly Jerusalem.

- As it journeys with Jesus, the assembly reaches out to the world with the good news of the kingdom of God and gathers followers who will travel with the people of God on the way to the feast. Thus, you have a special opportunity to emphasize the missionary nature of the church and muster the gifts of the assembly for the evangelization of the world.

Lent

Lent is that time in the liturgical year when the community "prepares with joy for the paschal feast" (Preface, Lent I). Notice the word *joy*. Lent is a joyful season because we are going up to the feast. This means that Lent is paschal in character; its focus is the passover of the Lord.

On this last leg of its journey to the paschal feast, the assembly seeks to renew itself wholly. The celebration of passover, after all, is not an empty ritual; it engages the assembly in the death of Christ so that it might rise with him in glory. Each year the assembly's challenge is to give its life more fully to the glory of God.

The elect (those chosen for Christian initiation) are joined to the faithful on this Lenten journey. Step by step, and supported by the Christian assembly, they make their way to the sacraments that draw them into the great passage.

Suggestions

- From the beginning of Lent, draw the assembly's attention to the Easter Triduum. As a community, whatever we do in Lent for the preparation of the elect and for the renewal of our own lives is for the sake of our fullest participation in the feast.
- Always speak of the community's journey to the feast. Lent is a time when we travel together as the people of God.
- Keep in mind that the liturgy of the word is the primary place where the church's renewal occurs. The community needs to hear and take to heart the great gospels of the season. Your preaching should lead the assembly into a renewed commitment to Christ, a more vibrant witness in

the eucharistic prayer, and a more profound covenant with the Lord in holy communion. Then, at the great feast, the assembly will be able to give itself to God in the fullest possible way; it will enter into the joy of the Lord.

The Easter Triduum

The Triduum is the heart of the liturgical year and the centre around which all its times and seasons turn.

For your preaching, it's important to remember that this three-day festival is a single feast, shot through from beginning to end with the glorious passover of the Lord.

Suggestion

- Unify the three-day festival with your preaching. Even while you highlight one or another aspect of the passage, keep the entire mystery before the eyes of the assembled church.

Easter Season

The festival of Christian Passover overflows into a fifty-day celebration of the victory of Jesus Christ. These fifty days are traditionally called "Great Sunday." We celebrate them as a single feast of unrestricted joy. In fact, the season should move forward with increasing joy until it reaches its grand culmination on Pentecost Day.

Suggestions

- Before you begin to preach during the Easter season, it's a good idea to take a careful look at all the sets of Sunday readings. You will notice that, although there is a particular thrust to the readings on the feasts of Ascension and Pentecost, the Sunday readings tend to celebrate the resurrection, ascension and gift of the Spirit as a unitive event.
- During the other times and seasons of the liturgical year, the homilist needs to draw the readings into the core of the good news. Notice the difference here. The readings of the Easter

season are right at the centre of the Christ-event. This will have quite an influence on your preaching.

- The Easter season is the prime time for drawing the assembly into the inner meaning of their participation in the sacred mysteries. With the neophytes or newly-initiated Christians in the assembly, and with the readings announcing the victory of Christ, you have a special opportunity to unfold the significance of the church's sacramental events.

In Summary

1. The liturgical year is a principal element of the church's spiritual life. It structures our paschal journey to the fullness of the kingdom of God. Always take it into account when you prepare your homilies.

2. Every season and time has a particular accent and flavour. Before you begin preaching in a new part of the liturgical year, reflect on its authentic spirit and its connection with the paschal mystery of Jesus Christ.

Discussion Questions

1. The liturgical year is the framework of the church's journey to the fullness of the kingdom. How would you draw greater attention to the church's journey in your preaching?

2. The homily is profoundly theological; again and again it reveals the mystery of salvation. How does the homily differ from theological catechesis or instruction?

That Our Hearts Might Burn

In the final chapter of his gospel, Luke tells us a remarkable story. On the day of Jesus' resurrection, "the first day of the week," two of Jesus' disciples were walking to Emmaus, some seven miles west of Jerusalem. They were despondent and confused. As they were on their way, "Jesus himself came near and went with them," although they did not recognize who he was. As far as they could tell, he was just another pilgrim returning from the feast.

Jesus opened the scriptures for them (the first homily?): "Then beginning with Moses and all the prophets, he interpreted to them the things about himself in all the scriptures." When they reached the village, the disciples urged Jesus strongly to stay with them, and when they were at table the disciples recognized him in the breaking of the bread. "Then their eyes were opened, and they recognized him, and he vanished from their sight. They said to each other, 'Were not our hearts burning within us while he was talking to us on the road, while he was opening the scriptures to us?"

Luke was a masterful writer, and we may assume that he had more than meets the eye in mind. Surely he was giving us a picture of the church that is valid for all time.

Our Own Easter Walk

Today we are the company of disciples; and today we are on an Easter walk, a journey home. On "the first day of the week," we too come together as we travel; and (surprise!) the Lord is in our midst. He opens the scriptures to us: "He is present in his word, since it is he himself who speaks when the holy Scriptures are read in the Church" (*Constitution on the Sacred Liturgy*, 7). And he presides at the breaking of the bread. Such is the extraordinary setting of the homily in the church's eucharist!

- The goal of the homily then becomes clear. It is to break open the word so that the disciples may see once again how the scriptures are accomplished in the Lord's passage and how they are filled out in us this very day.
- Put another way, the goal of the homily is to build us up as the community of the good news, to help us stand in awe before the mighty works of God, to open our eyes to the wonder of the moment, to let us recognize the presence of the Lord and the salvation he brings us here and now, to make us more fully church, to allow us with one voice to say "Amen!" to God.
- The homily takes us beyond evangelization, beyond catechesis and instruction, beyond a scientific study of the sacred texts, beyond all moral admonitions. It takes us into the heart of the mystery that we celebrate today. It fills us with joy. And it makes the church a faithful witness: "That same hour they got up and returned to Jerusalem ... Then they told what had happened on the road, and how he had been made known to them in the breaking of the bread."

GLOSSARY

Assembly: derived from the Latin *ecclesia* meaning assembly of citizens or church. The church is the new assembly of the world convoked by the Lord.

Catechesis: from the Greek *katechein*, to echo, follows evangelization and the reception of initial faith. It strengthens the acceptance of the good news and fills out the great story of salvation as it has been held by the apostolic church throughout the ages.

Chair: an original part of the church's liturgy. The bishop or presbyter presides from the chair during the liturgy of the word and from the table or altar during the liturgy of the eucharist. The chair is highly symbolic; it is the teaching chair of Jesus Christ and the apostles. The title cathedral (from the Latin *cathedra*, chair) designates the location of the diocesan episcopal chair.

Evangelization: from the Greek *evangelion* and the Latin *evangelium*, good news, gospel; refers to the first work of the church, namely the preaching of the gospel to those who have not yet heard it or received it in faith.

Homily: from the Latin *homilia*, conversation or discourse; is the ongoing proclamation of the good news within the church's official assemblies. Suggests a familial kind of discourse.

Mystery: from the Greek *musterion*; refers to something that is hidden from sight. In New Testament usage, however, it expresses the eternal plan of God for our salvation, once hidden but now made manifest in the passage of Jesus through death and resurrection to exalted kingdom life. Thus the term "paschal mystery."

Paraclesis: from the Greek *parakalein*, to invoke, to summon; the ongoing proclamation of the good news in the midst of the gospel community itself. Its purpose is to build up and summon anew the witness of the church.

Paschal: from the Hebrew *pesah* and the Latin *pascha*, passage or passover; refers to the passage of the Lord through death to the life of glory.

Preside: from the Latin *prae* + *sedere*; to sit in front of or at the head of (an assembly). The bishop or presbyter is the president of the church's official assembly. He presides as the sacramental icon of Christ.

Sermon: from the Latin *sermo*, speech or conversation; came to be identified as a religious discourse within, but not part of, the liturgy itself. The devolution of the homily into a sermon may be connected with the church's use of large basilicas for its celebrations. When the presidential chair became too remote for preaching, the bishop removed his chasuble and walked down into the body of the church. He then ascended a narrow staircase wrapped around a pillar to a box-like ambo and delivered his homily there. Thus the bishop's discourse was eventually interpreted as an action separate from the liturgy itself.

BIBLIOGRAPHY

Recommended Reading

Bonneau, Normand, o.m.i. *The Sunday Lectionary: Ritual Word, Paschal Shape*. Collegeville: The Liturgical Press, 1998.

_____ *Preparing the Table of the Word*. Ottawa: Novalis and Collegeville: The Liturgical Press, 1997.

Edwards, Paul, SJ. *The Practical Preacher*. Collegeville: The Liturgical Press, 1994.

Fulfilled in Your Hearing: the Homily in the Sunday Assembly, Bishops' Committee on Priestly Life and Worship, National Conference of Catholic Bishops (U.S.A.), 1982. This is the most useful and up-to-date document on the homily available today. It can be found in *The Liturgy Documents* (Liturgy Training Publications: Chicago, 1991).

Fuller, Reginald. *What is Liturgical Preaching*? London: SCM, 1957. Fuller's foundational exposition of liturgical preaching is developed in the first chapter of this present volume. His book, currently out of print, is available in theological libraries.

Skudlarek, William, O.S.B. *The Word in Worship*. Abingdon Press: Nashville, 1981. An excellent treatise on liturgical preaching.

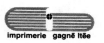
imprimerie gagné ltée